COOL CASTLES

CONTENTS

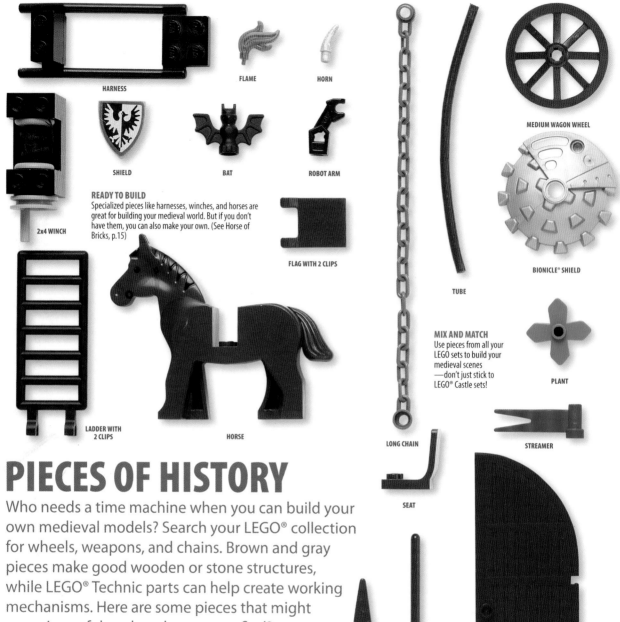

HARNESS

FLAME

HORN

SHIELD

BAT

ROBOT ARM

MEDIUM WAGON WHEEL

READY TO BUILD
Specialized pieces like harnesses, winches, and horses are great for building your medieval world. But if you don't have them, you can also make your own. (See Horse of Bricks, p.15)

2x4 WINCH

FLAG WITH 2 CLIPS

BIONICLE® SHIELD

TUBE

MIX AND MATCH
Use pieces from all your LEGO sets to build your medieval scenes —don't just stick to LEGO® Castle sets!

PLANT

LADDER WITH 2 CLIPS

HORSE

LONG CHAIN

STREAMER

SEAT

PIECES OF HISTORY

Who needs a time machine when you can build your own medieval models? Search your LEGO® collection for wheels, weapons, and chains. Brown and gray pieces make good wooden or stone structures, while LEGO® Technic parts can help create working mechanisms. Here are some pieces that might come in useful—what else can you find?

4x8 DOOR

4x6x3 ROLLCAGE

TAIL

TORCH

SWORD

SPEAR

LANCE

MEDIEVAL WEAPONRY
Your minifigures can wield weapons—or you could incorporate them into your models as traps or defensive features. (See Siege Tower, p.23)

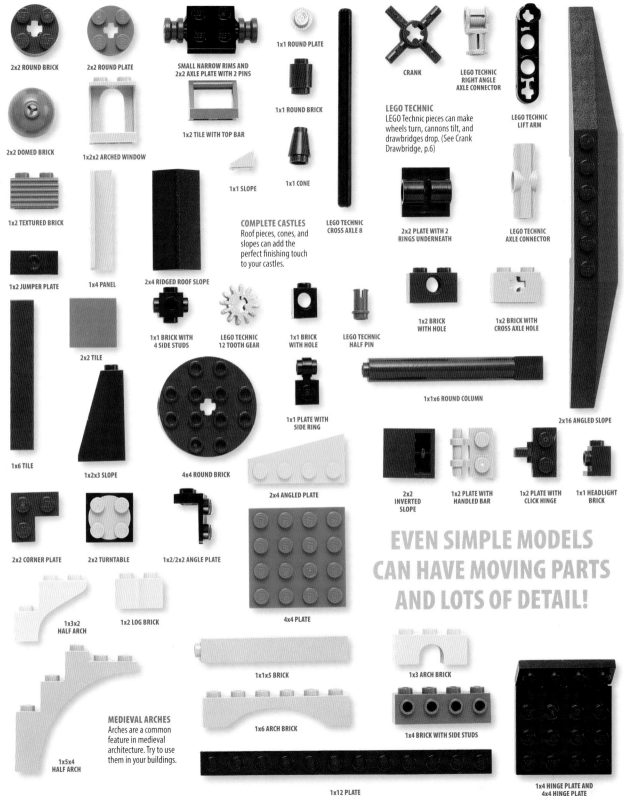

2x2 ROUND BRICK

2x2 ROUND PLATE

SMALL NARROW RIMS AND 2x2 AXLE PLATE WITH 2 PINS

1x1 ROUND PLATE

1x1 ROUND BRICK

1x2 TILE WITH TOP BAR

1x1 SLOPE

1x1 CONE

CRANK

LEGO TECHNIC RIGHT ANGLE AXLE CONNECTOR

LEGO TECHNIC LIFT ARM

2x2 DOMED BRICK

1x2x2 ARCHED WINDOW

LEGO TECHNIC
LEGO Technic pieces can make wheels turn, cannons tilt, and drawbridges drop. (See Crank Drawbridge, p.6)

1x2 TEXTURED BRICK

COMPLETE CASTLES
Roof pieces, cones, and slopes can add the perfect finishing touch to your castles.

LEGO TECHNIC CROSS AXLE 8

2x2 PLATE WITH 2 RINGS UNDERNEATH

LEGO TECHNIC AXLE CONNECTOR

1x2 JUMPER PLATE

1x4 PANEL

2x4 RIDGED ROOF SLOPE

1x1 BRICK WITH 4 SIDE STUDS

LEGO TECHNIC 12 TOOTH GEAR

1x1 BRICK WITH HOLE

LEGO TECHNIC HALF PIN

1x2 BRICK WITH HOLE

1x2 BRICK WITH CROSS AXLE HOLE

2x2 TILE

1x6 TILE

1x2x3 SLOPE

4x4 ROUND BRICK

1x1 PLATE WITH SIDE RING

1x1x6 ROUND COLUMN

2x16 ANGLED SLOPE

2x4 ANGLED PLATE

2x2 INVERTED SLOPE

1x2 PLATE WITH HANDLED BAR

1x2 PLATE WITH CLICK HINGE

1x1 HEADLIGHT BRICK

2x2 CORNER PLATE

2x2 TURNTABLE

1x2/2x2 ANGLE PLATE

4x4 PLATE

EVEN SIMPLE MODELS CAN HAVE MOVING PARTS AND LOTS OF DETAIL!

1x3x2 HALF ARCH

1x2 LOG BRICK

1x1x5 BRICK

1x3 ARCH BRICK

MEDIEVAL ARCHES
Arches are a common feature in medieval architecture. Try to use them in your buildings.

1x6 ARCH BRICK

1x4 BRICK WITH SIDE STUDS

1x5x4 HALF ARCH

1x12 PLATE

1x4 HINGE PLATE AND 4x4 HINGE PLATE

CASTLE

Medieval castles are huge, sturdy structures. Other than that, you can build your model however you want: grand, ornate, plain, strong, majestic, or crumbling. You could even build it as a combination of all these things! Look at pictures of ancient castles, or find inspiration in your favorite books and movies. Think about including details like flags, wall-mounted torches, and knight minifigures to bring your creation to life.

BUILDING BRIEF

Objective: Build medieval castles

Use: Home for royalty and knights, defending the village, location of jewels and treasure

Features: Must be big and strong, able to withstand attack, majestic architecture

Extras: Interior rooms, inner courtyards, drawbridge, moat, gardens, a whole town within the castle walls

CASTLE FORTRESS

Castles are built up over time as each king or queen adds what he or she needs. Start with an impressive doorway and a grand central building. Then add on sections to house sleeping quarters, viewing platforms, dining rooms, chapels, stores, and anything else you can think of. They don't even have to match!

Different sections can be built from different materials. Use brown bricks for wooden walls and gray for stone

Log bricks are great for medieval building

ARCHITECTURE

An interesting architectural feature can really give your model a boost. Here, a smaller arch has been built in behind a larger arch, which adds depth and detail to the chapel walls. Cones, round bricks, and round plates are stacked to make decorative columns. Be inventive!

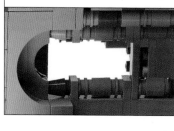

Some parts of the castle can be very ornate, even if others are plain. Cones, tiles, and side stud pieces can create imposing sculptures

CURVED BATTLEMENTS

Rounded battlements can help your knights keep a lookout in all directions. Use hinged plates to connect several sections of wall together. Then angle the walls into a circle, semicircle, or whatever shape you want.

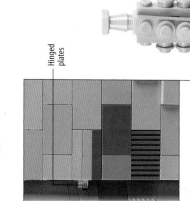

Hinged plates

Fly flags in your army's colors. You could also display shields or printed tiles to identify your king or queen

This castle even has a chapel attached

Arched windows. If you haven't got arched bricks, use half arches or inverted slopes

Arrow slits made from bricks with cross axle holes

A green brick here and there looks like a moss-covered stone!

Bricks in different shades of gray, textured bricks, and log bricks help break up large stone walls

Green baseplate is a good starting point, but why don't you try building your castle on a hill, or on an island in the middle of a lake?

Scattered plates and tiles look like fallen ruins

Overgrown foliage suggests an old castle. You could build a well-tended garden instead

Imposing entrance. You could also add a gatehouse with a way to keep invaders out! (See pp.6–9)

Wooden structures with lattice windows look really medieval!

DRAWBRIDGES

Every castle needs protection from invading armies. First build a simple gatehouse as an imposing front to your fortification. Then, think about how best you want to defend your castle and design a mechanism to suit. You could create a portcullis, a heavy stone door, or a drawbridge. Here are two clever ways to build a drawbridge!

Crank controls drawbridge

OPEN   **CLOSED**

GATEHOUSE

A simple gatehouse can be the first point of protection for your castle. Gray bricks and LEGO Technic half pins on either side of the door attach the drawbridge.

Make sure the doorway is high enough for a knight to ride through on horseback!

LEGO Technic half pin allows drawbridge to pivot

Push lever to release gears and send drawbridge crashing down!

MEDIEVAL MECHANISM

LEGO Technic gears turn to raise the lift-arms. These pull the chains, raising the drawbridge. A lever secures the drawbridge in place by locking an axle connector against the gears.

CRANK DRAWBRIDGE

A crank system is a simple way to raise and lower a drawbridge. This mechanism is housed in a stone battlement that connects to the top of the gatehouse. It uses LEGO Technic bricks, axles, and gears that allow you to operate the drawbridge using a crank on the side of the building.

Make drawbridge wide enough to cover entrance when raised

Drawbridge raised by chains attached to lift-arms

CABLE DRAWBRIDGE

There's more than one way to raise a bridge! This version of the gatehouse uses a spool and string cable system instead of chains and lift-arms. The mechanism is housed in a rustic-style gatehouse room.

CLIPPING THE CABLES

Use plates with handled bars to secure your drawbridge's cables. Thread the cable through both handles before clipping them to the underside of the drawbridge.

Winch

Hand-cranked winch is not as fast as a gear system, but it gets the job done!

SPOOL SYSTEM

The cables are attached to a winch inside the gatehouse, which is turned by a handle on the outside. This system takes up little space, which leaves room in the gatehouse for guards and ammunition.

Not enough gray bricks? Build the top of your gatehouse using wood colors instead!

Use a brick with cross axle hole in it to feed the cables through

Winch

CLOSED

OPEN

Don't have LEGO Technic parts? Use hinged bricks or plates to build a movable drawbridge

Plate with handled bar

PORTCULLIS

A portcullis is a heavy gate that can be raised and lowered on a pulley system. It is another great way to let friends into your castle—and keep enemies out! Start with a simple gatehouse like the one on the previous page, and adjust it to house your portcullis.

AW. THANKS TO THAT PORTCULLIS, WE NEVER GET TO BATTLE ANYBODY ANYMORE!

BUILDING BRIEF
Objective: Build portcullises for your castle
Use: Keeping intruders out
Features: Portcullis that can raise and lower easily
Extras: Gatehouse, defenses

Put knights and soldiers on top to defend gatehouse

One-brick-wide channel between two layers of the front wall

Tall gatehouse tower leaves room for portcullis to slide all the way up

Decorative windows built with 1x1 round bricks, plates, and small arches

GATE GAP

Build two layers into the front wall of the gatehouse, leaving a narrow channel between them. Drop the portcullis into this gap before building the roof, so it is trapped inside the gatehouse, but able to slide up and down freely.

PORTCULLIS

This portcullis is built from crisscrossed long, thin plates, with no special pieces needed. A string attached to a plate with handled bar at the top raises it through a channel created by the space between the two layers of the front walls.

Display your castle's coat of arms on the gatehouse walls. You could also fly flags or hang weapons!

NO ONE GETS IN UNLESS THEY KNOW THE PASSWORD!

BRICKS IN THE WALL

To add realistic textures to a stone wall, include textured bricks and log bricks among regular bricks, or attach 1x2 tiles to pairs of headlight bricks so they protrude from the wall.

When portcullis is closed, brick at end of drawstring sits on top of the tower

Plate with handled bar attaches string to door

To raise gate, pull brick down and attach it to top of archway, holding portcullis in place

REALLY? OK... THE PASSWORD IS "LET ME IN OR ELSE!"

PORTCULLIS LOWERED

You could also put a portcullis behind your castle's front door!

Portcullis moves smoothly because nothing blocks its way

PORTCULLIS RAISED

CASTLE DOORS

When building a door for your castle, think about what it's for. Royal processions and grand entrances? Then make it really big and fancy! To keep out unwanted guests, make it sturdy and strong with a way to lock it from inside. Or perhaps you'd like a secret door to protect a room full of treasure? It's all up to you!

DOOR OF DANGER

The door to a villain's castle should say "keep out!" to any heroes who approach. This simple door is made from standard bricks and tiles and attaches to the frame with clips and handled bars.

A bat or a flaming torch would look just as scary here!

Rattling chain hints at the spooky danger waiting inside

Use pieces with unusual or dramatic shapes to make creepy decorations

UNHINGED

Build the doors of this creepy entrance first. Next, construct the doorframe around them so you can position the clip pieces correctly.

Horn pieces warn intruders to keep out. You could also use tooth plates or tools

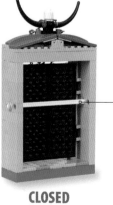

OPEN **CLOSED**

Locking mechanism—a LEGO Technic cross axle slides through a brick with a hole through it to lock the door

No welcome mat here!

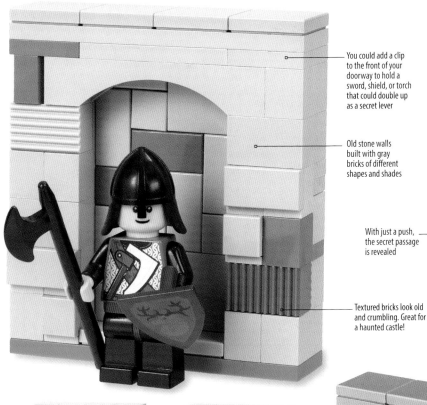

You could add a clip to the front of your doorway to hold a sword, shield, or torch that could double up as a secret lever

Old stone walls built with gray bricks of different shapes and shades

With just a push, the secret passage is revealed

Textured bricks look old and crumbling. Great for a haunted castle!

SECRET DOOR

The trick to building a secret door is to make it blend in with the castle's wall. First build an arched doorway with two clip plates at the back. Then design your door to match!

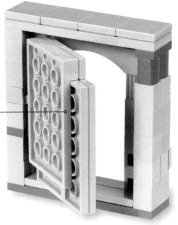

REAR—OPEN

FRONT—CLOSED

FRONT—OPEN

Plates with horizontal clips hold door in place and form the hinge

DOOR DESIGN

Just a few basic plates form the foundation of the door. Cover them with tiles that match the color and design of the tiles around the doorframe. Now your door will be camouflaged! Make sure there's enough space around the door for it to swing open smoothly.

Plate with handled bar secured with overlapping pieces

TRAPS

To build up your medieval scene, why not add some extra detail to your castle? Perhaps your castle has hidden treasure, which needs protecting from thieves. Or maybe you'd rather design a clever way to trap your enemies. Design some sneaky traps to keep your secrets safe! Adding moving parts to your models really brings them to life!

BUILDING BRIEF
Objective: Build medieval traps
Use: Fun with moving parts
Features: Spinning, dropping, or chopping mechanisms
Extras: Mazes, dungeons

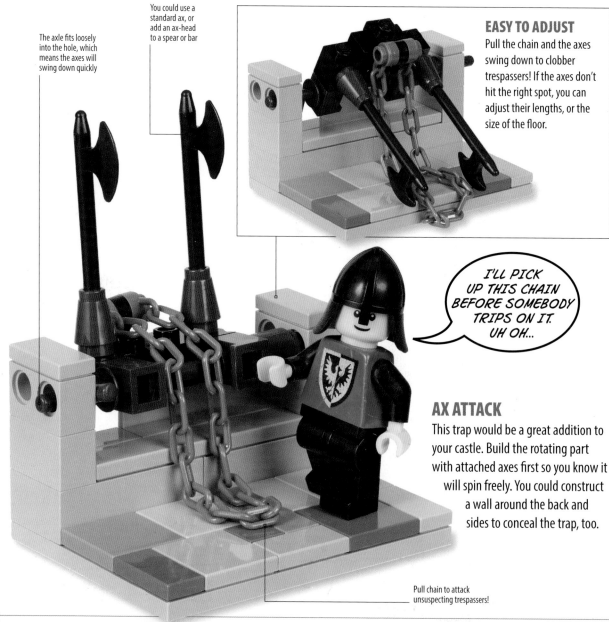

The axle fits loosely into the hole, which means the axes will swing down quickly

You could use a standard ax, or add an ax-head to a spear or bar

EASY TO ADJUST

Pull the chain and the axes swing down to clobber trespassers! If the axes don't hit the right spot, you can adjust their lengths, or the size of the floor.

I'LL PICK UP THIS CHAIN BEFORE SOMEBODY TRIPS ON IT. UH OH...

AX ATTACK

This trap would be a great addition to your castle. Build the rotating part with attached axes first so you know it will spin freely. You could construct a wall around the back and sides to conceal the trap, too.

Pull chain to attack unsuspecting trespassers!

TRAPDOOR

A trapdoor needs to swing down to drop people out of sight, so build it up high. The door should match the rest of the floor (whether wooden or stone) so it's a huge surprise for unsuspecting minifigures!

WHAT A GREAT VIEW. NOW, HOW DO I GET DOWN?

Two lance pieces support the door. One acts as a hinge, while the other can be pulled out to send the door swinging down.

Railing—you could also add stairs

Stopper keeps trap door from swinging too far

Build this platform into your castle's floor to include it in your medieval scene!

Trapdoor built separately from the rest of the platform

Extra piece on end of trap-release pole for better grip

Lance fits loosely in holes so the trap swings open easily

A minifigure who fell through the trap...a long time ago!

13

KNIGHTLY STEEDS

What's a knight without his faithful horse? On foot, that's what! Many LEGO Castle sets include horses, but you can also build your own. It's simple to give each horse its own individual character! Build and customize special saddles and horse armor, also known as barding. You can even build your knight's armor to match!

> **BUILDING BRIEF**
> **Objective:** Make horses worthy of a knight!
> **Use:** Riding forth for deeds of derring-do
> **Features:** Must be interesting and colorful
> **Extras:** Coat of arms, plumes, pennants, weapon and shield clips

Don't have plume pieces? You could use flames, feathers, or Viking horns!

NOW THIS IS WHAT I CALL RIDING IN STYLE!

Helmet has holes for plumes and other decorations

Swap the sword for a lance when it's time for a jousting tournament!

Armor comes in many colors and styles. Choose something that matches your army's colors

Chain makes horse look tough and armored

You could also add a horse battle helmet to protect your steed

Barding built from angled plates and tiles. Use different plate shapes to create unique saddle designs

MOUNTED KNIGHT

The only buildable surface on a LEGO horse is where the rider's feet attach. So to make your own barding, you'll need to build out from there. Clip and bar plates can help you build in two directions.

Flag pieces make good barding, too!

Use different colors to build up your army's identity

You can use a LEGO saddle or build your own!

MY HORSE IS TOTALLY OFF THE CHAIN!

1x1 plate with horizontal clip

This clips to 1x1 plate with horizontal clip on saddle

A tile locks the plates together without adding too much bulk

Two-toned coat, created by mixing classic and modern brown bricks. Create your own patterns!

Ears made from 1x1 cones

You could make the bricks around the gap a different color to resemble a saddle

Hooves made from round black bricks

HORSE OF BRICKS

If you don't have a horse for your knight, try building one! This brick-built horse has a gap to fit a minifigure. Its body is built from simple bricks and plates, with a few slopes and inverted slopes.

WAGONS & CARTS

Every medieval villager needs a trusty horse-drawn wagon to get them to the market. Before building your cart or wagon, think about what you want it to carry: food, equipment, passengers? You could even make an armored battle-wagon with lots of spears and spikes!

....
BUILDING BRIEF
Objective: Create carts and wagons
Use: Travel, transportation
Features: Pulled by horse, carry supplies
Extras: Lanterns, repair tools, horse food

WOODEN WAGON

This wagon has plenty of room for carrying supplies from town to town. Build the part that attaches to the horse first to ensure everything is the right height and all four wheels touch the ground to roll evenly.

Many wagons have smaller front wheels than back wheels

BOTTOM VIEW

Simple hood shows that driver is a peasant, not a knight or king

OFF TO THE MARKET WITH A LOAD OF FRESHLY PICKED BRICKS!

Driver's seat stays stationary while front wheels turn

Wooden boarding, built from brown tiles. You could use bright colors for a festive painted wagon

Make sure wheels aren't blocked by back of wagon when it turns

If you don't have a LEGO horse, try building your own! (See p.15)

TURNING THE WAGON

As the horse changes direction, it turns the front axle, which pulls the rest of the wagon along behind. You can use different pieces to make a turning wagon, from a turntable to a LEGO Technic pin.

Round brown plate is attached to a turntable, allowing front axle to turn

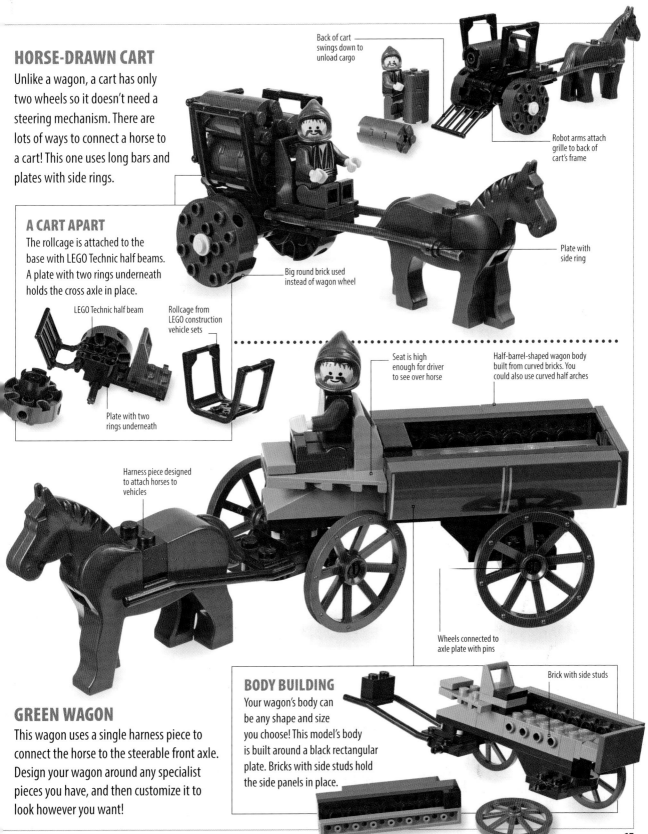

HORSE-DRAWN CART

Unlike a wagon, a cart has only two wheels so it doesn't need a steering mechanism. There are lots of ways to connect a horse to a cart! This one uses long bars and plates with side rings.

Back of cart swings down to unload cargo

Robot arms attach grille to back of cart's frame

A CART APART

The rollcage is attached to the base with LEGO Technic half beams. A plate with two rings underneath holds the cross axle in place.

Big round brick used instead of wagon wheel

Plate with side ring

LEGO Technic half beam

Rollcage from LEGO construction vehicle sets

Plate with two rings underneath

Seat is high enough for driver to see over horse

Half-barrel-shaped wagon body built from curved bricks. You could also use curved half arches

Harness piece designed to attach horses to vehicles

Wheels connected to axle plate with pins

BODY BUILDING

Your wagon's body can be any shape and size you choose! This model's body is built around a black rectangular plate. Bricks with side studs hold the side panels in place.

Brick with side studs

GREEN WAGON

This wagon uses a single harness piece to connect the horse to the steerable front axle. Design your wagon around any specialist pieces you have, and then customize it to look however you want!

DRAGONS

No medieval world is complete without a fierce, fire-breathing dragon. Dragons are mythical creatures, so there are no rules about what they should look like. Give yours spikes, fangs, horns, tails, chains, curves, and as many wings as you like! What else can you think of?

BUILDING BRIEF
Objective: Create terrifying dragons
Use: Protecting your castle, attacking enemies
Features: Large wings, sharp fangs, fiery breath, movable limbs
Extras: Dragon caves, baby dragons, saddles for a minifigure rider

FLYING SERPENT

This lean, agile dragon has a twisted body built from lots of LEGO Technic parts. Its back is shaped and held together with ball-and-socket joints, while axles and LEGO Technic half beams make up the front arms.

Don't have these horn pieces? Use screwdrivers, daggers, or bars —anything long or pointy will do!

Horns face backward so dragon is streamlined when flying

Neck joint is not fixed in place so the head can be posed as you like

ALL IN HIS HEAD

The dragon's head is built in four different directions. The bottom part has studs facing up, the sloped sides are built outward to the left and right, and the inside of the mouth has a jumper plate facing forward, which holds the flame piece in place.

Printed angled slopes add detail

Angle plates allow sideways building

Jumper plate faces forward

I MIGHT BE MADE OF HEAT-RESISTANT PLASTIC, BUT I'M STILL SCARED!

Use joints to create posable ankles and knees

Build the shape of your dragon using ball-and-socket joints

Can your minifigure tame the dragon?

Dragons don't have to have feet! Why not build some claws instead?

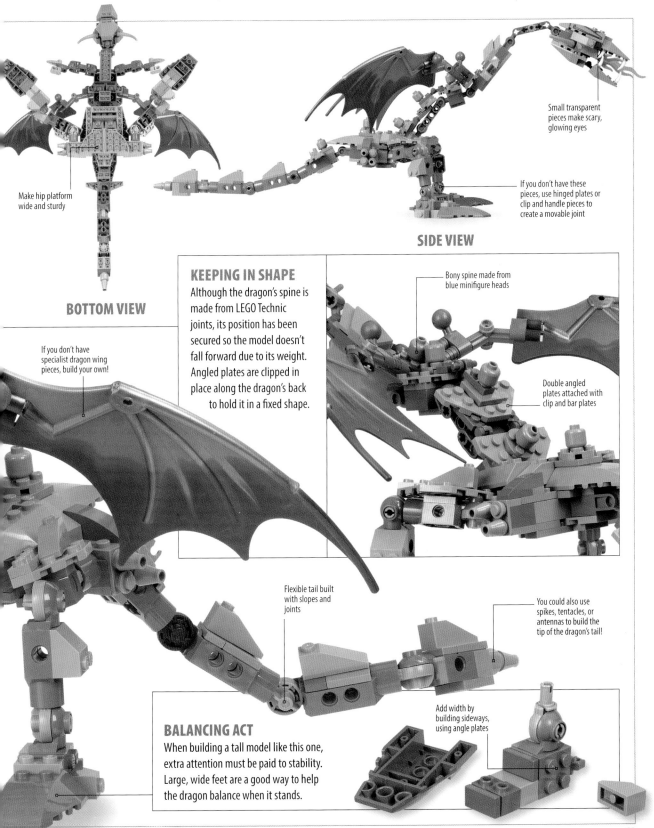

Small transparent pieces make scary, glowing eyes

Make hip platform wide and sturdy

If you don't have these pieces, use hinged plates or clip and handle pieces to create a movable joint

SIDE VIEW

BOTTOM VIEW

If you don't have specialist dragon wing pieces, build your own!

KEEPING IN SHAPE

Although the dragon's spine is made from LEGO Technic joints, its position has been secured so the model doesn't fall forward due to its weight. Angled plates are clipped in place along the dragon's back to hold it in a fixed shape.

Bony spine made from blue minifigure heads

Double angled plates attached with clip and bar plates

Flexible tail built with slopes and joints

You could also use spikes, tentacles, or antennas to build the tip of the dragon's tail!

BALANCING ACT

When building a tall model like this one, extra attention must be paid to stability. Large, wide feet are a good way to help the dragon balance when it stands.

Add width by building sideways, using angle plates

BATTERING RAMS

A battering ram is like a medieval tank: heavy, tough, and almost unstoppable. It needs a sturdy frame and a strong, swinging ram that can smash through your enemy castle's best defenses. It needs a set of wheels too, so your LEGO knights can move the huge contraption around!

BUILDING BRIEF
Objective: Build battering rams
Use: Breaking through the fortifications of enemy castles
Features: Strength, stability, swinging mechanism
Extras: Wheels, shields, armor plates, flags

SWING AND SMASH

A swinging mechanism is built into this ram's support frame. The castle's attackers stand behind the ram, pull it back as far as they can, and then let go. Gravity and momentum take care of the rest!

Axles at the top and bottom of the lift arms let battering ram swing back and forth freely

Battering ram hangs from two pairs of LEGO Technic lift arms

You could also use wagon wheels for a lighter, faster battering ram

Swinging hinge made from LEGO Technic cross axle and bricks with holes

Make the frame as sturdy as you can with overlapping bricks

Angle plates attach sides to the base

I LOVE THE SOUND OF CASTLE GATES CRASHING DOWN IN THE MORNING!

Silver plates look like bolted metal to hold heavy loads

REAR SIDE VIEW

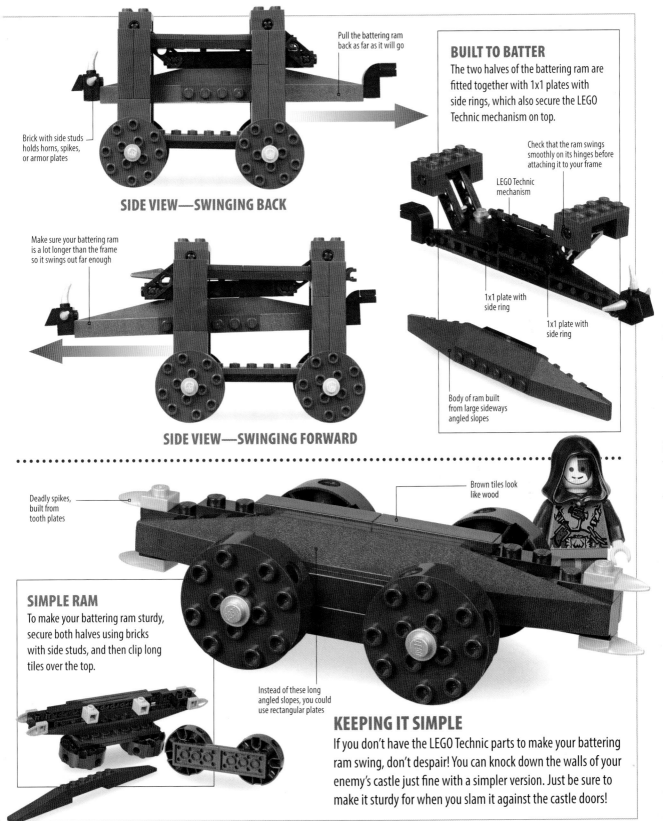

Pull the battering ram back as far as it will go

Brick with side studs holds horns, spikes, or armor plates

SIDE VIEW—SWINGING BACK

Make sure your battering ram is a lot longer than the frame so it swings out far enough

SIDE VIEW—SWINGING FORWARD

BUILT TO BATTER

The two halves of the battering ram are fitted together with 1x1 plates with side rings, which also secure the LEGO Technic mechanism on top.

Check that the ram swings smoothly on its hinges before attaching it to your frame

LEGO Technic mechanism

1x1 plate with side ring

1x1 plate with side ring

Body of ram built from large sideways angled slopes

Deadly spikes, built from tooth plates

Brown tiles look like wood

SIMPLE RAM

To make your battering ram sturdy, secure both halves using bricks with side studs, and then clip long tiles over the top.

Instead of these long angled slopes, you could use rectangular plates

KEEPING IT SIMPLE

If you don't have the LEGO Technic parts to make your battering ram swing, don't despair! You can knock down the walls of your enemy's castle just fine with a simpler version. Just be sure to make it sturdy for when you slam it against the castle doors!

LAYING SIEGE

Laying siege to an enemy castle is no easy task!
You can build all kinds of equipment for your
army of knights. A portable shield will protect
them from spears and arrows as they advance
across the battlefield, while a tall siege tower
will help them climb over the castle walls.

Use gray bricks to create
a stone wall—but
remember, a stone wall
wouldn't be portable!

Cones at top create
the look of wooden
poles bound together

PORTABLE SHIELD

Offering protection
for knights on the
move, this shield wall
is made by alternating
1x2 log bricks with 1x1
round bricks. This structure
makes the wall flexible enough
to bend into a curve.

IT'S LIKE A GAME OF HIDE AND GO SEEK... READY OR NOT, HERE WE COME!

Siege army is safe and
sound behind the wall!

Rolling wheel rims
allow knights to push
wall toward castle

Plate with click hinge

ROLLING WALL

The portable shield rolls
on small wheel rims
without tires. You can
attach a horse to the
click hinge at the
front to tow the wall
to the battlefield!

Wheel rim

REAR VIEW

SIEGE TOWER

A siege tower is like an armored ladder for reaching the top of enemy walls. This one is built on a rectangular plate and has a drawbridge-like gangplank to deposit the knights onto castle walls.

ER...DID I MENTION I'M AFRAID OF HEIGHTS?

Spears intimidate the enemy. You could also use flags to declare victory

Folded-up gangplank protects knights until they reach castle wall

Spears attached through the hole in headlight bricks

Hinged plate allows gangplank to be raised and lowered

Bricks in different shades of brown look like the tower is built from scraps of wood

Overhanging plate underneath gangplank stops it from lowering too far

Make sure wheels are positioned so the tower doesn't topple over

DRAWBRIDGE CLOSED

Knights climb up ladder or take shelter inside open back of tower

HOLLOW INSIDE

The back of the siege tower is left open so that the knights can hide inside. A ladder is clipped on to two of the side spears. It can be folded out to allow the knights to climb up it.

REAR VIEW

CANNONS & CATAPULTS

Siege weapons are designed to throw objects at or over a castle's walls. Beyond that, the only limit is your imagination! So be creative and keep an eye out for parts that would work as catapult buckets or cannon barrels. And remember—don't aim anything at your eyes!

BUILDING BRIEF

Objective: Build siege weapons
Use: Attacking castle walls and towers
Features: Ability to throw, fling, or launch projectiles
Extras: Wheels, guards, spare ammo wagons

TILT TO AIM

This cannon can be tilted up and down thanks to a few LEGO Technic pieces. The barrel is built around two bricks with holes, through which is fitted a cross axle.

Axle allows cannon to tilt

Brick with a hole

Barrel made from 2x2 round bricks with a domed brick at the back

Frame uses LEGO Technic parts so the barrel can move up and down

BOTTOM VIEW

MICROCATAPULT

The basic components of a catapult are a bucket attached to an arm and a sturdy base to support them. With a rotation point in the middle of the throwing arm, this catapult works like a see-saw.

Rotation point

Radar dish for bucket

Push this end down, and the other goes up!

Wagon wheels make a heavy cannon more portable

MICROCANNON

For a siege on a smaller scale, you can make a microcannon. This model is built out of two LEGO Technic tubes, supported by headlight bricks.

ASSEMBLE YOUR WEAPONS!

The LEGO Technic tubes are connected by a plate with horizontal clip, which attaches to the headlight bricks with 1x1 round plates.

1x1 round plate

Plate with horizontal clip

Torch made from a flame piece and robot arm

THIS CANNON IS SURE TO GO WITH A BANG!

CANNON

Official LEGO cannons can be found in many ship sets. If you don't have one, though, just build your own! You need a long barrel, a base, and some wheels if you want to make it mobile.

MICROMEDIEVAL

Have you ever wanted to build a really big castle, but didn't have enough bricks? Try shrinking it down! Build it at a smaller-than-minifigure scale to make huge structures from just a few bricks. Your LEGO knights might not fit inside, but with the right pieces and some imagination, you can create churches, houses, animals—even a whole micromedieval world!

BUILDING BRIEF
Objective: Build microscale castles and other microcreations
Use: Building up a medieval world
Features: Tiny but easily identifiable
Extras: A whole surrounding kingdom

FANTASY CASTLE

This magical castle may be small, but it has plenty of interest. A small arch is used to top the front gate, a tile can be a drawbridge, and round 1x1 bricks make the towers. The roofs are covered in 1x1 dark gray slopes, cones, and tiles to complement the sand-colored walls.

Make your castle as elaborate as you want!

TOP VIEW

Columns built with 1x1 round bricks and plates

Drawbridge is a single tile supported by plates

A 1x1 cone makes a great tree at microscale!

Castle roof made from ridged roof slopes

Square windows are actually the backs of headlight bricks

Arched window

STONE CASTLE

For a traditional-looking castle, start with a few plates to make a base. Next, add the corner towers and then build the rest of the castle between them. Pointy roofs, arched doors, and thin walls complete the look!

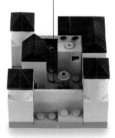

Tree made from 1x1 round brick

TOP SIDE VIEW

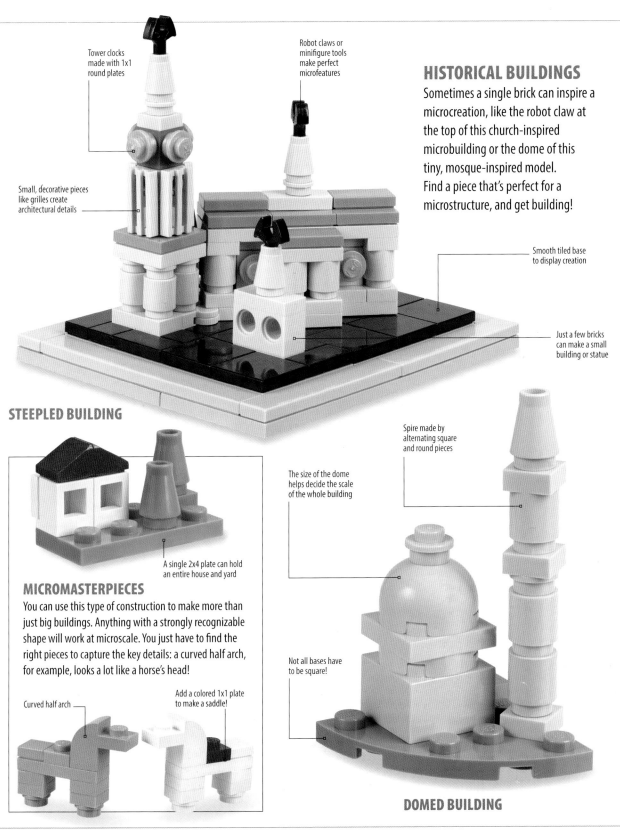

Tower clocks made with 1x1 round plates

Robot claws or minifigure tools make perfect microfeatures

HISTORICAL BUILDINGS

Sometimes a single brick can inspire a microcreation, like the robot claw at the top of this church-inspired microbuilding or the dome of this tiny, mosque-inspired model. Find a piece that's perfect for a microstructure, and get building!

Small, decorative pieces like grilles create architectural details

Smooth tiled base to display creation

Just a few bricks can make a small building or statue

STEEPLED BUILDING

Spire made by alternating square and round pieces

The size of the dome helps decide the scale of the whole building

A single 2x4 plate can hold an entire house and yard

MICROMASTERPIECES

You can use this type of construction to make more than just big buildings. Anything with a strongly recognizable shape will work at microscale. You just have to find the right pieces to capture the key details: a curved half arch, for example, looks a lot like a horse's head!

Not all bases have to be square!

Curved half arch

Add a colored 1x1 plate to make a saddle!

DOMED BUILDING

DK | Penguin Random House

Editor Shari Last
Additional Editors Jo Casey, Hannah Dolan, Emma Grange,
Matt Jones, Catherine Saunders, Lisa Stock, Victoria Taylor
Senior Editor Laura Gilbert
Designer Owen Bennett
Additional Designers Lynne Moulding, Robert Perry,
Lisa Sodeau, Ron Stobbart, Rhys Thomas, Toby Truphet
Jacket Designer David McDonald
Senior Designer Nathan Martin
Senior DTP Designer Kavita Varma
Producer Lloyd Robertson
Managing Editor Simon Hugo
Design Manager Guy Harvey
Creative Manager Sarah Harland
Art Director Lisa Lanzarini
Publisher Julie Ferris
Publishing Director Simon Beecroft

Photography by Gary Ombler,
Brian Poulsen, and Tim Trøjborg

Acknowledgments
Dorling Kindersley would like to thank: Stephanie Lawrence, Randi Sørensen, and
Corinna van Delden at the LEGO Group; Sebastiaan Arts, Tim Goddard, Deborah
Higdon, Barney Main, Duncan Titmarsh (www.bright-bricks.com), and Andrew
Walker for their amazing models; Jeff van Winden for additional building; Daniel
Lipkowitz for his fantastic text; Gary Ombler, Brian Poulsen, and Tim Trøjborg for
their brilliant photography; Rachel Peng and Bo Wei at IM Studios;
and Sarah Harland for editorial assistance.

First published in the United States in 2015 by DK Publishing
345 Hudson Street, New York, New York 10014

Contains material previously published in
The LEGO® Ideas Book (2011)

001—284611—Mar/15

Page design copyright © 2015 Dorling Kindersley Limited.
A Penguin Random House Company.

LEGO, the LEGO logo, BIONICLE, the Brick and Knob configurations, and the
Minifigure are trademarks of the LEGO Group. © 2015 The LEGO Group. Produced by
Dorling Kindersley Limited under license from the LEGO Group.

A catalog record for this book is available from the Library of Congress.

ISBN: 978-5-0010-1305-1

Printed in China.

www.dk.com
www.LEGO.com

A WORLD OF IDEAS:
SEE ALL THERE IS TO KNOW